COMBUST MOBIL FOR PLYMOUTH

SUSTAINABLE TRANSPORT GROUP
CLIMATE ACTION PLYMOUTH

David Bricknell
with Pat Bushell, Michael Littledyke, Ricky Lowes, and Tony Staunton.
Supporting contributions from Alyson Smith and Ian Poyser

August 2021

SUMMARY

The Sustainable Transport Group of Climate Action Plymouth consider that, in order to meet Plymouth's stated Climate Emergency aims within a vibrant economy, vehicle traffic must be 'Combustion Free'. Transport derived Global warming Greenhouse Gas (GHGs) emissions and toxic emissions are the product of the combustion of fuel.

A three-pronged approach of increasing walking, increasing cycling, and removing combustion vehicles and replacing them with zero-emission transport is recommended – none of these solutions will be successful alone.

The success of the walking/cycling/Electric Vehicle approach depends upon making active travel faster, cheaper and more convenient than using a combustion vehicle and ensuring its safety by physically segregating pedestrian areas from cycling lanes, and cycle lanes from normal vehicle traffic.

We recommend

- significantly increasing the amount of pedestrian-only areas and widening pavements at the expense of road space in order to encourage more active travel and to provide for safe physical-distancing whilst doing so;

- extending and prioritising cycle routes to ensure cycling is both quicker and more convenient than vehicle transport. Cycle lanes must be segregated from pedestrian and vehicle traffic in order to enhance safety sufficiently to encourage new cyclists as well as ensuring the safety of existing cyclists;

- incentivising zero-emission vehicles (principally Battery Electric Vehicles BEV) whilst disincentivising combustion engine vehicles, both actions to apply to private, commercial and public transport. Funds raised from disincentives for combustion vehicles can be used directly to fund incentives for BEVs.

Our longer-term vision for Plymouth is for a community formed around pedestrian neighbourhoods with prioritised walking and cycling connected by an integrated public and private zero-emission transport network.

Buchanan report on Traffic in Towns, 1963

"Cars are a boon. But they have now started to choke movement and, indeed, to threaten the quality of urban life."
Buchanan offers two main ideas for re-planning towns.
First, main traffic should be canalised into a 'primary road network'. Here traffic takes precedence.
Second, the rest of the town should be planned as 'environmental areas'.
As a majority of voters would soon become car owners, politicians would be 'anxious to please the motorist and frightened of annoying him' making 'drastic action politically difficult' [1]

_____

Decarbonising surface transport

There are two ways to decarbonise surface transport: Switch to non-carbon fuels (electric, hydrogen); and reduce traffic volumes. - Dr Steve Melia, Senior Lecturer Transport and Planning in the Centre for Transport and Society UWE Bristol. [2]

_____

Changing the cars that we drive

"We have to change the cars we drive, and the only way to do that is to change the new cars. We can't change used ones" - Christina Bu of the Norwegian EV Electric Vehicle Association. [3]

_____

The effects of COVID-19

"It is important to put this on the table: this virus may become just another endemic virus in our communities, and this virus may never go away," - Michael Ryan, the WHO's emergencies chief.

Transport Secretary Grant Shapps - statement 9th May 2020 [4]

Even with public transport reverting to full service - once you take into account the 2-metre social distancing rule – there would only be effective capacity for one in ten passengers on many parts of the network.

... when the country does get back to work, we need those people to carry on cycling and walking, and to be joined by many more.

Otherwise, with public transport capacity severely restricted, more cars could be drawn to the road and our towns and cities could become gridlocked.

... pedestrians will need more space.

.. there's been a 70% rise in the number of people on bikes whether it's for exercise, or for necessary journeys.

Pop-up bike lanes. Wider pavements. Cycle and bus-only streets.

..
So, to help keep this quiet, clean car revolution going, I can also announce today, £10 million of additional support for car-charging points on our streets.

Plymouth has applied for and been awarded £249,000 for an emergency active travel fund in response to the COVID-19 pandemic. PCC will apply for a further £995,000 in phase two for more permanent schemes.

The fund will create a temporary segregated cycling link from the rail station through Armada Way to a new pop-up cycle parking facility at the Guildhall. The scheme will also include increased cycle parking at Milehouse park and ride, new 20mph zones at schools, the removal on unnecessary barriers on pavements and cycle lanes, and steps to tackle parking in cycle lanes.[5]

Abbreviations

ABP	Associated British Ports
ANPR	Automatic Number Plate Recognition
BEV	Battery Electric Vehicle
CH	Hydrocarbons
CH4	Methane
CHC	Cattewater Harbour Commissioners
CO	Carbon Monoxide
CO2	Carbon Dioxide (GWP=1)
CEV	Combustion Engine Vehicle
COMEAP	Committee On the Medical Effects of Air Pollution
COPD	Chronic Obstructive Pulmonary Disease
DPF	Diesel Particulate Filter
ECA	Emission Control Area
FAQ	Frequently Asked Questions
FUD	Fear, Uncertainty, Doubt
GDI	Gasoline (petrol) Direct Injection
GHGs	Green House Gases
GRT	Gross Registered Tonnage
GWP	Global Warming Potential
HFC	Hydroflourocarbons
LFP	Lithium Iron (Ferrous) Phospate
Li-Ion	Lithium Ion Battery
LMO	Lithium Manganese Oxide
LNG	Liquified Natural Gas
LTO	Lithium Titanate Oxide
MARPOL	International Convention for the Prevention of Pollution from Ships
MPA	Marine Protected Area
MCA	Maritime and Coastguard Agency
MCZ	Marine Conservation Zone
NCA	Nickel Cobalt Aluminium
NMC	Nickel Manganese Cobalt
NMHC	Non-Methane Hydro-Carbon
NO	Nitrous Oxide
NOx	Nitrogen Dioxide (principally)
PM	Particulate Matter
Ro-Pax	Roll-On Vehicle / Passenger Ferry
QHM	Queen's Harbour Master
SAC	Special Area of Conservation
SCR	Selective Catalytic Reduction
SECA	Sulphur Emission Control Area
SOx	Sulphur Oxides
SPA	Special Protection Area
SUV	Sports Utility Vehicle
Scrubber	Exhaust gas wash
TECF	Tamar Estuaries Consultative Forum
μm	micro metre

Table of Contents

THE CLIMATE EMERGENCY AND AIR QUALITY CRISIS

1. The Climate Emergency and Air Quality Crisis

1.1 The **Climate Emergency** identifies the crisis faced by all humanity caused by the accelerating increase in average global temperatures. The speed of temperature increase from the growing levels of Green House Gases GHGs has not been previously experienced throughout human history.

1.2 Global Warming arises due to GHGs from Transport, Energy, Business, Residential, Industrial, Public, and Agriculture. Shipping and Aviation are not captured in official statistics but need to be. [6]

1.3 **"(Plymouth City) Council has declared a climate emergency"**. This means that we [PCC] are working with our partners to make Plymouth 'carbon neutral' by 2030. The 2030 target stems from the Intergovernmental Panel on Climate Change (IPCC) 2018 report which outlined the impact of a temperature rise in excess of 1.5 degrees Celsius." The report stated that urgent action was required tackle climate change. [7]

1.4 "'**Carbon Neutral**' is achieved by calculating the carbon footprint and then reducing it to zero through a combination of projects on efficiency measures and external emission reduction projects." [8]

1.5 We have less than 10 years to reduce GHGs sufficiently to prevent a rise of over 1.5°C. A rise of this magnitude will see an ice-free arctic, half of land and sea creatures severely affected, and a greater frequency of deadly heatwaves and severe flooding. On our current trajectory the rise to between 2.6 to 3.9°C would be catastrophic for the world as we know it – a world unliveable in for the human race. [9]

1.6 Great Britain has made significant steps in reducing greenhouse gas emissions – a 38% reduction since 1990 [10]. This has come about largely from a change from coal to gas and renewables - the rush to gas is still continuing[11]. Unfortunately, much of the reduction has been offset by an increase in imported CO_2 emissions from our increased reliance on goods from China [12].

1.7 Transport contributed to the reduction in CO_2 due to a reduction in miles driven and more efficient vehicles. However, vehicles are now getting bigger and less efficient, and COVID response may mean that miles driven begins to increase again due to reduced public transport use.

1.8 England lags behind Scotland in its ambition to reduce its impact on global warming.[13]

1.9 **Air quality** presents a connected but different challenge with up to 15m UK citizens at risk from toxic emissions and particulates. Transport is the major contributor to this. [14]

1.10 The recent announcement to bring forward the ban on all new sales of fossil fuel cars, including hybrids, by 2035, brought forward from 2040, is a sign that some level of realisation of the scale of the challenge, both in climate change and air quality, may be occurring but the motor industry questions the credibility of any plans behind the ambition.[15]

1.11 An ambitious zero-emission vehicle sales programme will still leave around half of the total vehicles on the road being combustion-powered in 2030.

1.12 Walking and cycling, as well as providing significant health and wellbeing improvements, must also be increased in order that the remaining combustion vehicles can be taken off the road, and that means creating space for more active travel.

1.13 Year 2020 saw the epidemic of SARS-COV-2 or COVID-19 become a pandemic affecting all our social interactions, the way we work, the way we enjoy our leisure and the way we travel. COVID-19 is now endemic, just as influenza and the common cold are. The mobility changes we make now are likely to become permanent, or at best be with us for quite some time.[16] Now is the time to introduce changes in the way we move around.

1.14 PCC has produced an **Action Plan for Mobility** covering immediate actions, actions to be assessed, and those requiring national support. There is a clear ambition to reduce GHG emissions, but Climate Action Plymouth believes that more could and must be done if **Plymouth City Council is to achieve net zero carbon emissions by 2030.**

1.15 Being a coastal city and major port, Plymouth is affected by both land transport and marine transport – wind direction and the extent of shipping have a significant impact on air quality.

1.16 This report addresses Transport (or Mobility), which is now the largest contributor of GHGs in the UK.

1.17 Mobility includes walking and cycling; local, national and international public or shared transport – taxis, buses, trains, planes, ferries, cargo and other boats and ships; and personal transport - cars, vans, lorries and sailing and motoring.

1.18 When considering mobility, to counter climate change from global warming and to improve air quality, it is necessary **to prioritise active-travel including walking and cycling, to open spaces for safe socially-distanced mobility and, where vehicle traffic is necessary, to stop burning fossil fuels and to deliver Combustion Free Mobility.**

SUMMARY ACTIONS

2. Summary Actions

2.1   Climate Action Plymouth believes Plymouth City should:

2.1.1   encourage walking by introducing more pedestrian friendly zones physically separating pedestrians from cycle and vehicular traffic;

2.1.2   introduce car-free days (perhaps every Sunday or every other Sunday) particularly in the historic and shopping centres, expanding the area covered to reflect their popularity;

2.1.3   free Plymouth's historic waterfront from traffic. Madeira Road, Southside Street, The Parade, Exchange Street and Quay Road would all benefit from being pedestrian areas. Access to Elphinstone Car Park could be retained;

2.1.4   keep pavements clear of obstacles and penalise pavement parking;

2.1.5   introduce car-free and/or 20mph zones around schools and hospitals;

2.1.6   consider a '20-minute neighbourhood' planning objective;

2.1.7   introduce more cycle routes prioritised over motor transport and physically segregated from pedestrians and vehicle traffic;

2.1.8   consider how best to integrate electric scooters into the transport system;

2.1.9   consider bicycle, electric bikes, and electric scooter hubs strategically placed to encourage people out of the cars and to move around the city actively and cleanly;

2.1.10 Incentivise last-mile delivery and collection by bicycle power;

2.1.11 consider High Occupancy (2+) Lanes, to encourage an increase in the number of passengers per personal vehicle;

2.1.12 incentivise the use of zero emission cars and light vans including free parking, access to bus and high occupancy lanes, and free bridge and ferry tolls coupled with increasing the number of free-to-use chargers;

2.1.13 provide a number of rapid EV charger hubs around the city;

2.1.14 provide on-street EV charging without the need to use car parks or other restricted entry sites;

2.1.15 provide interest-free loans for battery electric taxis whilst maintaining the fossil-fuel price per mile together with free charging from city centre charge points;

2.1.16 progressively ban the most polluting vehicles from the city centre based Euro emission standards – Euro 1, 2, 3 & 4 before the end of 2020, Euro 5 by end 2022, Euro 6 by 2025;

2.1.17 progressively phase out 'last mile' deliveries by fossil-fuel light vans, transitioning to zero-emission deliveries within the city;

2.1.18 disincentivise high CO_2 vehicles (>100g/km) entering the city centre according to CO_2 emissions;

2.1.19 provide an integrated non-franchised public transport system offering free transport for key workers and those in need;

2.1.20 accelerate the introduction of a zero-emission battery electric fleet of buses and its supporting charging infrastructure.

2.1.21 step up pressure to electrify the mainline rail system adopting battery power where necessary including in tunnels, in order to reduce the line upgrade costs

2.1.22 consider how Plymouth could participate in the coming electric aviation;

2.1.23 introduce and enforce a low (air and water) emission zone in The Sound and Estuaries;

2.1.24 require all intra-harbour craft (ferries, tour boats and pilot craft, etc.) to be zero emission and provide the suitable charging infrastructure;

2.1.25 provide 'cold-ironing' shoreside charging for all international traffic, ferries, cargo, and cruise ships using the port of Plymouth.

2.1.26 consider how to sustain an integrated zero-emission public transport system covering all of Plymouth and its suburbs, accessible by all and providing regular and reliable transport throughout the day and night.

2.1.27 Consider making public transport free for essential workers with tickets transferable across providers.

2.1.28 Investigate a metro style electric rail system re-opening many of the old stations throughout Plymouth

2.2 In reducing or eliminating combustion from Transport, Plymouth will:

2.2.1 contribute towards the reduction in global warming through a reduction in GHGs, in particular CO_2;

2.2.2 provide cleaner air, free from the toxic emissions that have such a damaging effect on our population;

2.2.3 provide the space for safe and enjoyable active travel;

2.2.4 provide a more aesthetic, quieter, and less stressful environment with more opportunities for exercise and community involvement.

GREENHOUSE GAS AND TOXIC EMISSIONS

3. Green-House Gas and Toxic Emissions

Emissions arise principally from combustion of fossil fuels

3.1 Anthropogenic global warming is occurring due to the 'Greenhouse' effect of global warming gases in the atmosphere. The Global Warming Potential (GWP) of Greenhouse Gases (GHGs) include Carbon Dioxide CO_2 (GWP=1), Methane (~56x), and Nitrous Oxide NO (~280x) as well as Hydrofluorocarbons HFCs (up to 10,000x).[17]

3.2 When considering mobility, the prime focus is on reducing Carbon Dioxide CO_2 as a by-product of combustion whilst avoiding the potential shift to methane (or biomethane) which, although it can sometimes be considered a 'renewable' fuel, has a significantly higher GWP whilst still contributing NOx.

3.3 Alongside reducing GHGs from reducing combustion must come the reduction of toxic emissions which will significantly contribute to improving air quality. Care should be taken when decreasing one not to inadvertently increase the other, as the UK diesel car promotion showed. GHGs affect climate change and toxic emissions primarily affect air quality.

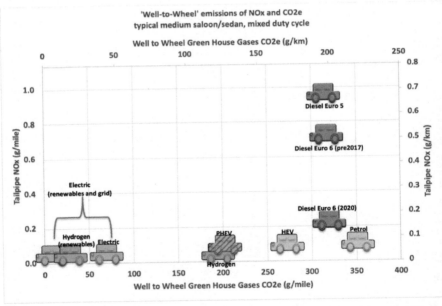

Tailpipe NOx and Well-to-Wheel CO_2 for typical mid-sized saloon car. For a double decker bus, CO_2 is about six times greater per mile and NOx an order of magnitude greater. [18] Average number of bus passengers is about nine making emissions for public transport and for personal vehicles about the same per passenger mile. [19].

3.4 Toxic emissions arising from the combustion of fossil fuels affect air quality and consist of two types – gases and particulates.

3.5 Toxic gases include carbon monoxide (CO), methane (CH_4), non-methane hydrocarbons (NMHC) and hydrocarbons (CH) and nitrogen oxides. NOx is the principal concern and is a direct hazard to health responsible for aggravating cardiovascular and respiratory disease.

3.6 NOx arises from combustion. Higher efficiency, lower CO_2 engines can produce greater amounts of NOx. Exhaust gas after-treatment is used to reduce NOx, usually by Selective Catalytic Reduction (SCR) where urea is introduced to the exhaust system with nitrogen, water and CO_2 the end products. An effective SCR will use urea in the proportion of about 1part urea to 14 parts fuel, something which anecdotally seems to be far from reality at the moment.

3.7 Sulphur Oxides (SOx) are a significant issue for international marine traffic, particularly if the operator chooses not to use low-sulphur fuel and instead uses Exhaust Gas Cleaning or 'scrubbers' to remove sulphur oxides from the exhaust and wash the highly acidic and corrosive wash-water directly into the sea.

3.8 Toxic particulates can penetrate deep into the lungs and fine particles can cross from the lungs into the blood stream, including crossing to the foetal side of the placenta.

3.9 Particulates are categorised as:

- PM_{10} (coarse 10µm to 2.5µm) these will reach into the upper respiratory tract,
- $PM_{2.5}$ (fine 2.5µm to 1µm) these will reach into the lower respiratory tract,
- PM_1 (inhalable 1µm to 0.1µm) these will reach deep into the alveoli, in the lungs where gas exchange takes place,
- $PM_{0.1}$ (ultra-fine <0.1µm) are the most hazardous and can reach into the bloodstream and whole body including crossing the placenta.

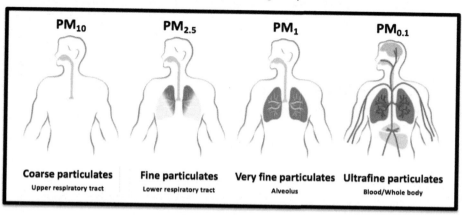

Penetration into the body of Particulate Combustion Emissions [20]

3.10   The finer the particle the more hazardous it is. "Exposure to particles can lead to mortality (death), increased admissions to hospital of people suffering from cardiovascular (heart) disease (attacks and strokes), and pulmonary (lung) disease, such as chronic obstructive pulmonary disease (COPD), bronchitis and asthma. Other compounds found on particulates, such as some hydrocarbons or metals, can cause cancer or poisoning [21]." The most recent evidence from the Government's Committee on the Medical Effects of Air Pollution (COMEAP) [22] suggests that some 29,000 deaths per year are brought forward by exposure to man-made particulate air pollution at current levels.

3.11   In transport terms, particulates arise from

- tyre, brake and road dust, generally described as PM_{10s} (although for Combustion Vehicles about 40% of brake wear, 70% of tyre wear, and 54% of road abrasion are $PM_{2.5}$). More research is underway. [23]
- the combustion process - generally described as $PM_{2.5}$ but having substantial amounts of very fine PM_1 and ultrafine $PM_{0.1}$.

3.12   With the introduction of Diesel and Gasoline (petrol) Particulate Filters (DPF and GPF) particle emissions from transport should all but be eliminated. However, any journey around town will cast doubts on this.

3.13   Diesel and now Gasoline Particulate Filters DPF don't always catch many of these very fine and ultra-fine particles and, because of their very small size, they tend not to produce visible smoke whilst remaining suspended in the air for some considerable time.[24]

3.14   The particulate filter burn-off process, originally intended to be done passively on long motorway journeys out of town, is now often done actively within town (to stop filters from clogging) and can cause significant spikes in particle emissions. [25]

3.15   Tyre and brake particles can be substantially reduced by regenerative braking and smoother acceleration and deceleration, something that is a characteristic of electric vehicles. Road dust can only be reduced by vacuum as road washing seems to have a rather minimal effect. [26]

3.16   The UK had a stated intention to adopt the more stringent World Health Organisation (WHO) particulate emission standards rather than the existing EU standards despite failing to even achieve those. [27] This means an annual mean exposure level for $PM_{2.5}$ of $10\mu mg/m^3$ down from 25 and for PM_{10} a limit of $20\mu mg/m^3$ down from 40. Plymouth does not currently meet WHO levels of emission albeit it does meet current UK/EU levels in most places except Exeter Street and Mutley Plain. [28]

3.17   Ultra-fine particulates are a specific health concern but are not reported by current testing. [29] Some of Plymouth's sensors capture this data but don't report it.

3.18 Eliminating combustion by products associated with transport essentially means replacing the Internal Combustion Engine (ICE) with zero-emission transport - this will reduce both CO_2 and toxic emissions.

3.19 Improving the efficiency of the combustion engine invariably incurs an increase in toxic emissions and in controlling NOx. This can also lead to an increase in Particulates - addressing one can lead to increasing the other.

3.20 Except in very high concentrations, CO_2 is not toxic (brewers [30] and canaries [31] beware) and the effect is generally global and not localised. Toxic emissions (NOx particularly) are dose or concentration related and hence are localised in their effect.

3.21 Particulates are often treated as dose related when monitored even though there is no safe dose (despite WHO guidelines) but the impact is localised.

PLYMOUTH AIR QUALITY PLAN

4. Plymouth Air Quality Plan

According to the World Health Organisation, Plymouth has worse air quality than London. In a list of UK towns and cities, Plymouth was ranked sixteenth out of thirty-two towns tested. [32] [33]

4.1 Plymouth aims to reduce its carbon footprint by reducing its contribution of GHGs and, in doing so, also to improve its air quality. Plymouth includes the town and suburbs as well as The Sound and its estuaries.

4.2 Plymouth has three Air Quality Management Plans for Exeter Street and Mutley Plain either for NOx or Benzene or both, in order to meet EU/UK standards (not WHO). There are no management plans for particulates. [34]

4.3 Plymouth has a number of initiatives captured on the Plymouth.gov.uk site but there is little evidence that these are having any impact at all. These initiatives include:

   a. The Walkabout Initiative to raise awareness of the issue and increase walking and cycling.

   b. Greener Council Fleet - although no policy exists to implement it

   c. Promote alternative fuels and technologies – ad hoc basis (although grudging support and passive hostility might be a better way of describing it.)

   d. Tree Planting – policy in place

   e. Travel Planning (car sharing etc.)

   f. Safe routes to school

   g. Cycle facilities and routes

   h. Managing the Road Network – high occupancy lanes, restrictions of traffic, etc.

   i. Emissions Management – old polluting vehicle scrappage: no scheme in place

   j. Retrofit of buses and HGVs

   k. Cleaner taxis - no plans

   l. Enforce no idling – no plans in place

WALKING AND PEDESTRIANISATION

5. Walking and Pedestrianisation

Increasing walking and cycling will reduce emissions from other transport and create space for socially distanced travel

5.1   Whilst Plymouth town centre has some pedestrian priority areas and a covered pedestrian-only shopping mall, the historic centre is not particularly pedestrian friendly. With the exception of part of Armada Way and a small strip of New George Street, there are no pedestrian-only areas.

5.2   If we are to increase walking to reduce traffic, then Plymouth needs more pedestrian-only areas that are attractive to walk in and with no parked cars (parked on the road, on the pavement or half-on, half-off) or car parks within the zone.

Plymouth's Old Town Street proposed pedestrian zone (Photo PCC)

Madeira Road – a perfect spot for promenading and enjoying Plymouth's world class waterfront, free of traffic. (Photo Hoe Neighbourhood Forum/McCaren Architecture)

The Parade in Plymouth's historic centre, a perfect setting for al-fresco dining but is largely a car park (Photo David Bricknell)

5.3 Further pedestrianisation would be beneficial to increasing leisure walking, including enjoying the wider waterfront area whilst social distancing and eating al-fresco.

Plymouth's historic waterfront would benefit considerably from having more pedestrian areas including Madeira Road, Southside Street, The Parade, Exchange Street and Quay Road. Access to Elphinstone Car Park could be retained.

Persistent drive-through traffic on Plymouth's 'pedestrian prioritised' Southside Street leaves little room for shoppers and tourists. (Photo David Bricknell)

5.4 Pavements are kept very narrow in the older parts of the centre in order to prioritise vehicle traffic and to allow kerbside parking and are often blocked with bins or cars parked on the pavements, leaving little room for safe walking.

*Obstructed and narrow pavements in Plymouth's historic centre
(Photo David Bricknell)*

Pavement parking in Plymouth's historic centre (Photo David Bricknell)

5.5 PCC's Action Plan suggests a car-free day per year, but it is suggested that car-free Sundays (or alternate Sundays) would have a more significant impact although the area that is car-free may have to be limited in the short term. Madeira Road, Southside Street, The Parade, Exchange Street and Quay Road could be the first areas to trial!

PCC is to be commended for its improvements to West Pier. The newly modified pedestrian area allows for 'al-fresco' dining and provides some much-needed seating areas. Much more of this could be done in the historic centre. (Photo David Bricknell)

5.6 Car-free residential areas should also be explored - some of the UK's larger cities have implemented these to improve play opportunities for children and to increase community interaction. [35]

5.7 Several studies have shown how traffic affects children's play and how it can adversely affect the coherence and communications within communities. [36]

5.8 Car-free zones around schools and hospitals are also suggested - no school should be on a drive-through road and parking should be restricted within a certain distance at school pick up and drop off times.

5.9 Where car-free areas can't be established, introduce **enforced** 20mph zones, particularly near schools and hospitals but also in many residential areas.

5.10 A longer-term aim might well be the 20-minute Neighbourhood. The 20-minute neighbourhood is all about 'living locally'—giving people the ability to meet most of their daily needs within a 20-minute walk from home, with safe cycling and local transport options. Progress with this should be monitored. Melbourne in Australia are pursuing the 20-minute and Paris the 15-minute City. [37] Plymouth's downtown is surprisingly difficult to live in without having to drive somewhere for essentials!

CYCLING

6. Cycling

6.1   Cycling is gaining a new prominence in the emerging transport system.   During the pandemic lockdown, cycling substantially increased. It is hoped that the trend for people to adopt cycling as a key part of their transport solution will continue.

Cycling has increased substantially during the pandemic and is set to be a key transport mode for many more of us into the future. (Photo tejvanphotos CC BY 2.0)

6.2   Plymouth is interlaced with cycle routes extending through the city and out past the suburbs. However, 'signed' and traffic-free routes are poorly connected, with many of the cycle lanes being little more than parking areas.

Blocked cycle lanes impede uptake of cycling. Elburton Road cycle lanes are just a car park (Photo David Bricknell)

6.3 The Highway Code states – "Rule 140 Cycle lanes. These are shown by road markings and signs. You MUST NOT drive or park in a cycle lane marked by a solid white line during its times of operation. Do not drive or park in a cycle lane marked by a **broken white line unless it is unavoidable**." Plymouth does not appear to enforce the **'unavoidable'**.

6.4 Cycle lanes with broken white lines should all be converted to solid lines and parking withing the cycle lanes should be rigorously penalised.

6.5 Plymouth's Action Plan consists of a list of improvements but policing these routes to ensure they are clear of parked vehicles is essential to their success.

6.6 Stop-start cycle lanes and shared pavements do little to promote an increase in cycling. "We know that there are many barriers that prevent people taking to people power. For some, it's fear of traffic. Others simply find the car or bus more convenient."[38]

6.7 Cycle routes should be physically segregated from both pedestrian and vehicle traffic[39] – perceived safety is a key factor affecting uptake of cycling by groups other than the speed and fitness groups.

Segregated Cycle Lanes (Photo cosimo .chiffi CC BY-ND 2.0)

6.8 Pop up cycle lanes, wider pavements and traffic-free school streets are part of the Government's recommendations to allow social distancing in an endemic COVID-19 environment. Dedicated cycle roads with a good distance from vehicle traffic will encourage more cycling and reduce exposure to toxic exhaust pollution.[40]

6.9 Alternatives to segregation of cycle lanes by kerbs could be by raised cycle ways. This solution, in particular, would be suitable for narrow roads and for new routes.[41] Toxic emissions such as NOx and CO (Carbon Monoxide) are both heavier than air and so riders should be a little more isolated from vehicle toxic pollution.

6.10 Cycle routes should be prioritised over vehicle traffic (including buses) in order to provide faster and easier travel into, out of, and around Plymouth. Drivers will only give up their cars only if cycling provides a quicker and easier way of getting to their destination.

6.11 Plymouth is hilly and maybe not topologically friendly to novice cyclist, but other cities with similar topologies have higher cycle adoption than Plymouth indicating that topology isn't such a barrier as its often perceived to be.[42]

6.12 Electric battery-assisted cycles (PEDELEC) should help alleviate the limitations of some budding (and some older) cyclists.

6.13 Battery powered scooters, and other similar monocycles and hoverboards, are currently illegal to use on both roads and pavements within the UK - something that may change in the future - but if they are introduced the impact on pedestrians must be considered if walking is not to be discouraged. The Government is trialling rental electric scooters.[43]

6.14 The provision of electric bike and, when legal, electric scooter facilities at train and bus stations and at tourist hot spots such as the Barbican and the Hoe should further encourage combustion-free travel.[44]

Battery scooters and pedestrians don't mix safely but their use will grow quickly as evidenced by other cities around the world. (Photo Jim Sallis, CC BY-SA)

6.15   Bicycles are an excellent zero-emission last-mile and local delivery and collection vehicle, for many things including recycling and food waste.

Electric Delivery Bikes [45] (Photo stekelbes CC BY-NC-ND 2.0 and Sainsbury)

PRIVATE, PUBLIC AND SHARED TRANSPORT

7. Private, public and shared vehicle transport

7.1 Whilst the city centre should be prioritised for walking and cycling, Plymouth is too large a city to rely solely upon these modes of transport when considering the suburbs and wider catchment areas.

7.2 A zero-emission integrated public and private transport system is essential to the workings of any city but on its own just introducing more buses will not reduce GHG's or toxic emissions nor will they have much impact on vehicle congestion. [46]

7.3 Diesel-powered buses are just as polluting per passenger mile as combustion-powered personal vehicle transport. Buses produce around ten times as much NOx per litre of fuel and use substantially more fuel per mile than a personal vehicle but can carry more passengers. Emissions per transport mile are similar across all forms of combustion powered transport. [47]

Buses and Trams

7.4 Government advice (May 2020) during the first wave of the COVID-19 pandemic is that all other forms of transport should be considered before taking public transport.[48] That advice has lingered even whilst infection rates have reduced. High utilisation of public transport, whilst slowly rebuilding, is unlikely to return to pre-COVID levels anytime soon.

7.5 Whether a diesel bus is lower emission than a combustion car depends upon the utilisation or number of passengers carried. A double decker bus carries an average of 9.2 passengers[49] so there is little difference in emissions between a diesel bus and a single occupant diesel car. Both can be improved by increasing occupancy albeit the COVID-19 situation makes neither likely in the near term, the expectation being that buses can run at a tenth of capacity (about seven passengers for a double decker) [50] and lift sharing is to be discouraged for anyone other than same household occupants..

7.6 On balance, over the whole day, including when buses are running with few passengers at off-peak times and cars are just parked, there is probably little difference between any of combustion-engine transport modes whether that is car, bus or rail.

7.7 Given that utilisation (or passenger numbers) is critical to the emissions per passenger both for private combustion vehicles, and combustion-powered bus and rail transport, then pre COVID-19 days everything possible should have been done to increase the numbers of passengers per vehicle. Incentivising public transport through lower fares and transferable tickets between various transport providers (such as the Oyster Card scheme) should be considered. However, during the first COVID-19 wave everything was done to discourage the use of public transport except where it was essential – leave public transport only to those with no other means of transport.[51]

7.8   High Occupancy Lanes were a tried and tested scheme for many towns and cities for reducing congestion but are unlikely now to be a solution. Instead bus and taxi lanes could be opened for zero emission vehicles: this would not address congestion but would benefit emissions and air quality.

7.9   Plymouth had an electric tram system from 1899 but it started to reduce in capacity from the 1930s and was closed in 1945 - it was zero emission at the point-of-use, but it used dirty energy from Prince Rock's coal fired power station. Reintroducing a tram system running on rails with priority routes is the one mode of public transport which can attract motorists from their cars, much more so than adding buses. It may be expensive to introduce and pre-COVID might have been considered as the favoured long-term solution.

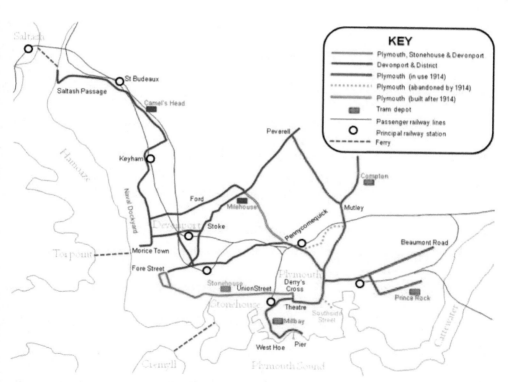

Plymouth Pre-War Tram routes.

Modern 'third-rail' tram system running through historic Bordeaux (Photo Andrew Batram by CC BY-NC-ND 2.0)

7.10 A trolley bus system, running on rubber and powered by overhead electric lines is less flexible, less efficient, with a higher capital cost that a battery-electric bus system but if route priority could be provided as with the tram system, then it might also have been an effective solution to shifting motorists from their cars to public transport.

7.11 Like all UK transport authorities except London (and most European countries), Plymouth's bus network today is privately franchise operated and as such is poorly integrated and expensive to travel on. [52]

7.12 Large conurbation Mayoral authorities today are pressing to reregulate local transport systems and undoubtably services have the potential to see significant improvements provided capital investment levels can also be significantly increased. [53]

7.13 London used their congestion charge fees to subsidise bus transport, initially to a level of about 50% of revenue raised [54]. Plymouth could consider something similar if they can find the revenue from some form of traffic charging, either emission or congestion based.

7.14 Car and van journeys account for around six times more journeys than public transport. Public transport improvements, without traffic restraint, make little difference to the habits of car drivers: they are more likely to generate additional trips, or to reduce walking or cycling. [55]

7.15 Doubling bus numbers leads to a reduction in car transport of about 1.3% and so is unlikely to impact much on GHG emissions whilst concentrating toxic emissions because most bus services are radial and travel in and out of the centre - places such as Oxford and Brighton can testify to this. [56]

7.16 Most of Plymouth's buses are diesel powered meeting Euro VI standards for toxic emissions whilst some achieve 30% less on GHGs. Some newer buses are gas fuelled (lower in CO_2 and in Toxic Emissions) but gas fuelled buses are only about 7% lower than a diesel fuelled bus for Greenhouse Gases. [57]

7.17 All combustion powered buses produce GHG and toxic emissions. [58]

7.18 Many countries and many cities within the UK are now using fully electric buses on a variety of routes. [59]

Plymouth trialling an all-electric bus. Over 150 of these buses operate in GB already.
(Photo RichardAsh1981 by CC BY-SA2.0)

7.19 Sydney, NSW, is replacing its entire 8000 buses with an all battery electric fleet. [60]

7.20 Plymouth is trialling a single battery electric bus. [61]

7.21 Over 150 electric buses, single and double decker, are in operation throughout the UK today. On Merseyside, for instance, the buses operate on routes of 100-130 miles per day for a duty cycle of 12 hours with some operating for up to 19 hours. No on-route charging is required. Depot charging can be done overnight at cheap off-peak rates – a substantial saving over diesel fuel costs. [62]

7.22 The Government has recently announced funding for all-electric bus towns and the introduction of zero-emission buses are essential before any expansion of bus services is undertaken. [63]

7.23 Most battery buses use cobalt-free Lithium Iron Phosphate (LFP) battery packs as opposed to battery cars which tend to use Nickel Manganese Cobalt (NMC) or Nickel

Cobalt Aluminium (NCA) batteries that use a small amount (in 2020 <10%) of cobalt in the cathode. (Consumer electronics use Lithium Cobalt Oxide LCO with cathodes that contain around 50% cobalt).

7.24 To replace the existing bus fleet will take some time and a depot charging infrastructure for 150 buses will need to be put into place. Once acquired, battery electric buses will be significantly cheaper to run on both fuel and maintenance whilst providing zero emissions at the point of use. [64]

Depot Charging for bus fleet (Photo Misanthropic One CC BY 2.0)

7.25 Other options to depot charging are available. Using Lithium Titanate Oxide (LTO) batteries in place of LFP allows 5-10 times higher charge rates, meaning charges of just a few minutes at certain stops make this a feasible mode of operation. LTO also exhibit very high cycle life albeit they are heavier for the same amount of energy. China has adopted this in a number of routes. [65]

7.26 Using supercapacitors in place of batteries allows extremely high re-charge rates coupled with very high cycle life. The Spanish company CAF have developed such a system in use in Seville. [66]

7.27 Particulates from brakes and tyres are significant from combustion vehicles but are much reduced on electric vehicles due to regenerative braking and smoother acceleration and de-acceleration.

Taxis

7.28   Most of Plymouth's taxis are diesel powered, and some are the misnamed 'self-charging' hybrids. There may be some Battery Electric Vehicles (BEV) taxis but none have been seen. Other cities have significant numbers of BEV taxis. Providing interest-free loans to purchase a BEV taxi, and holding the price charged for the ride to the same as a fossil fuel taxi should produce healthy margins for the driver due to significantly lower fuel and maintenance costs, making this highly attractive switch for the competitive taxi market.

7.29   Post COVID, the driver should be completely segregated from the passengers, more like the traditional Hackney Cab.

Electric taxis operating in many cities worldwide (Photo harr_nl by CC BY-NC-SA 2.0)

Rail

7.30   The rail system in the South West is diesel powered, not electric. Studies [67] indicate that diesel rail emissions are some 1.5 to 2 times higher per given distance than road traffic: per passenger comparison would depend upon both car and rail seat utilisation so a straight comparison is difficult. However, unlike an electrified rail system, diesel rail is certainly not low emission.

Electrified rail is essential to achieving a zero-emission public transport system.
(Photo Jimmy Harris CC BY 2.0)

7.31   Extending electrification to the South West is essential to reducing the climate impact and a high-speed rail link with the rest of the country would assist with further increasing rail adoption. It is recognised that electrifying the line from London to Bristol became very difficult due in part to the constrained dimensions of many tunnels. Thankfully, technical solutions to this challenge are now available by incorporating on-board batteries to enable run-through of areas difficult to electrify. Depending on the battery capacity, good distance and speed can be maintained. [68]

Private Cars

7.32 Private car transport dominates personal vehicle transport: 100 times more passenger miles are undertaken by private vehicles than by bus or coach. Within the timescale available to address climate change, public transport can only play a very small part and private car transport has to bear the largest burden![69]

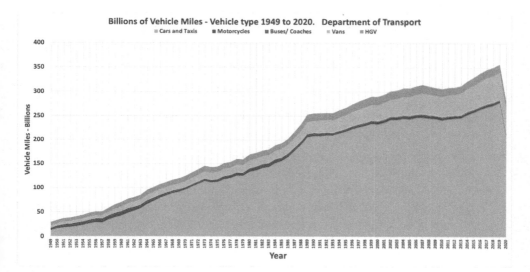

Billions of vehicle miles by traffic type 1949 to 2018 – Department of Transport

7.33 Post COVID-19, along with increased walking and cycling, private cars have to become the transport of choice as public transport will be running well below capacity for many years, and is, anyway, unlikely to be attractive enough to move car drivers to another form of transport in any reasonable timescale.

7.34 Almost all personal vehicle traffic in Plymouth is combustion powered and fuelled by either diesel or petrol; very few are gas fuelled. These Combustion Engined Vehicles (CEV) have a CO_2 impact as well as a toxic emission impact. Newer vehicles are cleaner than older vehicles, assuming they actually meet their required emission standards, but currently there are no restrictions on whether older vehicles meeting lower emission standards are allowed into the most traffic dense city centre.

7.35 London is now restricting older heavily polluting Euro 1, 2 and 3 Petrol vehicles and Euro, 1, 2, 3, 4, and 5 diesel vehicles from their Ultra Low Emission Zone ULEZ [70]. Many other cities are taking similar measures - older combustion engine cars can be up to ten times more polluting than vehicles meeting the latest standards.

7.36   Plymouth conducts emissions monitoring and considers that only Mutley Plain and Exeter Street currently regularly exceed allowable UK/EU emission levels. [71]

7.37   Whilst some cities do restrict combustion engine vehicles based on toxic emissions, none currently restrict based on CO_2. As CEVs have become more efficient, and fuel prices have remained low, cars have become bigger and heavier and hence produce greater levels of CO_2. [72]

7.38   The government approves cars based upon tested CO_2 emissions and hence, with Automatic Number Plate Recognition ANPR, restricting based upon CO_2 emissions is perfectly feasible – restricting these would, in particular, reduce the number of large Sports Utility Vehicle (SUV) type cars.

7.39   If we are to rely upon personal car transport then, as well as restricting many roads and areas to vehicle traffic and giving preference to active travel, all private vehicles must be zero emission and, in the timescale we have that means battery electric, as hydrogen is some way behind in technology development.

7.40   Sales of Battery Electric Vehicles (BEV) are gathering pace in the UK as more and more different models and manufacturers produce competitive versions. However, the current low-level of BEV sales are often masked by the number of Range eXtended Electric (ReX), Hybrid and Plug-In Hybrid Vehicles (PHEV) – ReX, Hybrids and PHEV will no longer be available for sale after either 2030/2035/2040 (depending on the Government's final decision).[73]

Annual market share – plug-in market share of new car registrations (2012 to date)

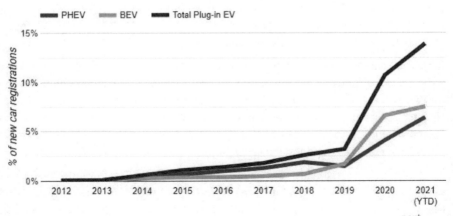

Source: SMMT, OLEV, DfT Statistics. Updated: May 2021

next
greencar

Plug-In market share – next green car

7.41   Achieving the end of new fossil fuel car sales by 2030 requires a very rapid increase in the sales of BEVs over the coming few years. Year 2020 and 2021 sales of EVs are very encouraging, with a very large uptick in sales.

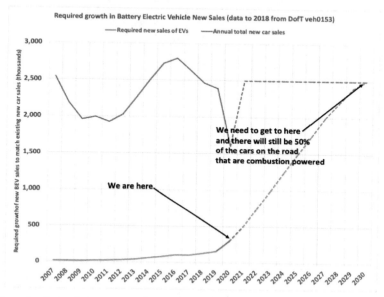

Required acceleration required in Battery Electric Vehicle sales to meet 2030 timescale – this will require national and local incentives

7.42   Even if all cars sold by 2030 were to be zero-emission these would still represent only about 40% of the total private cars on the road: replacing all fossil fuel cars would take until around 2040-2050.

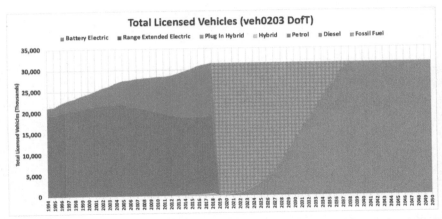

Even if all new car sales are BEV by 2030, it will take to nearly 2050 to replace all Combustion cars.

7.43   In 2020 when asked why people bought EVs, 47% said environmental reasons, 38% said running costs and a 5% stated technology. In the same study, reasons for not having an EV included higher initial costs and range limitation together with a lack of public charging stations given the time it takes to charge. [74]

7.44   Clearly, to ramp up from the February 2020 Year to Date UK BEV market share of 2.9% to an ambitious 100% zero-emission cars (mostly BEV) by 2030 will require significant incentives for BEVs both in purchase price, in taxation, and in ownership costs as well as significant disincentives for continued fossil fuel car purchases.

7.45   "We have to change the cars we drive, and the only way to do that is to change the new cars. We can't change used ones" - Christina Bu of the Norwegian EV Electric Vehicle Association. This means that to get 'affordable' BEVs into the second user market requires subsidies to new BEVs, including compact, family and executive vehicles. If we cannot accept this, for ideological reasons, then we will not achieve sufficient BEV uptake!

7.46   Private car sales make up about 42% of the total annual new car sales with business and fleet sales the other 58%.[75] Incentives for fleet and company cars is therefore essential.

7.47   Privately registered cars make up about 90% of the total cars on the road with business and fleet making up the other 10%: companies tend to keep cars for only 3 years, typically, whereas private cars can be on the road for some 10-15 years old, sometimes longer.[76]

7.48   Norway is the leader in EV sales through a combination of a clear direction of travel to control vehicle emissions (all new cars sold by 2025 should be zero-emission) and a number of attractive incentives of sufficient value to overcome any reticence to change from the known to the relatively unknown.

.49 **The incentives are paid for by disincentives on polluting cars so there is no loss in revenue.** [77]

.50 Norway's incentives include:

.50.1 Reduced initial costs through:

> a. No purchase tax (1990-)
>
> b. No import taxes (1990-)
>
> c. Exemption from 25% VAT on purchase (2001-), and on leasing (2015),
>
> d. 50% reduction company car tax (2000-2018), 40% reduction (2018-)
>
> e. Scrappage for fossil fuel cars (2018)

.50.2 Reduced running costs from:

> a. No annual road tax (1996-),
>
> b. No charges on toll roads or ferries (1997-2017).
>
> c. Max 50% on toll roads (2019).
>
> d. Max 50% on ferry fares (2018-)
>
> e. Free municipal parking (1999-2017),
>
> f. Max parking fee 50% (2018-)

.50.3 Driving priority benefits such as, access to bus and high occupancy lanes (2005) and, for some authorities the requirement for EVs to have 2+ occupants from 2016.

.51 In addition to purchase incentives, Norway has one of the widest differences in electricity prices compared to petrol/diesel prices. [78]

.52 The UK's EV incentives include:

.52.1 Purchase incentives

> a. A £3,000 plug-in grant for new EVs up to £50,000.[79] This has reduced from the £5000 available initially and subsequently reduced to £4,500, then £3,500.
>
> b. A six-year £35,000 interest-free loan (Scotland only)
>
> c. Zero Vehicle Excise Duty
>
> d. Exemption from the Luxury Car surcharge (April 2020-)
>
> e. Zero % Benefit in Kind (BiK) from April 2020 (company car)
>
> f. 100% First Year Capital Allowance (Company car)

.52.2 On running costs, company car drivers have

> a. no 'car fuel benefit in kind' charge,

b.   reduced national insurance contributions and

c.   cars are eligible for salary sacrifice schemes.

7.52.3 Driving priority benefits include free access to some clean air zones

7.53   Unfortunately, since the fuel duty escalator has not increased since 2010, fuel prices are historically low in the UK which has encouraged larger vehicles and more driving.

7.54   Post Covid-19 in 2020, fuel prices have further reduced by 20-30% substantially reducing the fuel cost advantage that BEVs enjoyed.

7.55   The number of Fuel stations peaked at around 37,539 in 1970. [80]. In 2019 there were 8,385 fuel stations in the UK in 2019, down from 13,107 in year 2000.[81] In some regions of the UK, rural areas of Scotland in particular, fuel stations are increasingly scarce with some drivers requiring journeys of 10 to 50-mile round trips to refuel, albeit refuel time once at the pump can be quite short.[82] As EV adoption increases this situation will be further exacerbated and 'range anxiety' will transition from BEVs to Combustion Engine Vehicles.

7.56   EV drivers do not consider Plymouth to be a very 'EV friendly' city. It has few chargers (7-22kW) and these are either sited at restricted sites such as hospitals or within expensive car parks. There is no on-street charging and only one public rapid (>50kW) charger and that is based in an expensive city-centre car park.

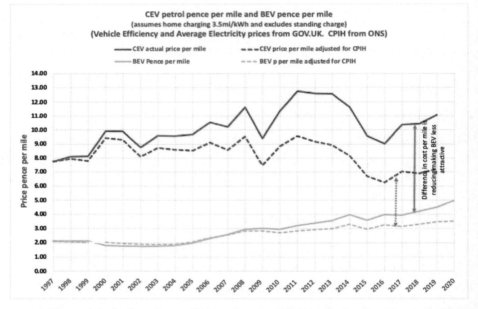

Difference in fuel cost per mile between Combustion Engine Petrol cars and BEV. Included is the adjusted cost for CPIH from a year 2000 baseline. In real terms 'Combustion Engine' motoring is significantly cheaper on fuel costs now than in 2000 whereas electricity costs continue to rise closing the gap between CEV and BEV.

7.57 BEVs are generally refilled quite differently to CEV depending on whether 'charging at home' is available. The 'ideal' charging regime is to plug-in overnight or, for commuters, during the day when not in use – this takes none of the driver's time, requiring no time queuing at pumps or time detouring to find a fuel station. For many drivers with a more recent longer-range BEV this will likely be the only charging they will ever need. BEV recharging can be quicker, easier and cheaper than fossil fuel.

7.58 Plugging in every day and allowing the car to stay for some time after completing the charge contributes to keeping the battery pack in tip-top condition as it allows the car to balance the multitude of battery cells within the pack. Some BEVS will have just 96 individual cells and some can have as many as 8,256. [83]

7.59 Home charging is the ideal arrangement for running a BEV and will enable a car with lower range to be selected in many instances. However, not all owners will have that ability. Apartment owners, terrace houses, and others, face a different but often not insurmountable challenge.

7.60 Plymouth's action plan identifies 100 new workplace chargers, six new car park chargers and up to 50 pop-up charge points in nine new charge hubs. However, on its own this does little to incentivise EV uptake. A snapshot of charging in Plymouth car parks midday one Friday showed only one EV plugged in. This should not be taken to indicate lack of demand but to show the hostile pricing environment presented to the EV driver.

Charging Rates			
Power Amps/kW	Maximum Miles per hour	Maximum km per hour	notes
AC Single Phase			
10A/2.3kW	7-9	11-15	UK 3-pin plug
16A/3.6kW	12-15	19-24	Slow
20A/4.5kW	15-19	24-30	Typical lamppost
32A/7.4kW	24-30	40-48	Fast
AC Three Phase			
48A/11kW	33-45	50-70	i3, Zoe, TM3&Y
96A/22kW	66-90	105-145	Zoe, (TMS&X 16.5kW)
186A/43kW	130-170	210-275	early Zoe, no longer used
DC			
44kW-50kW	132-200	212-322	CCS & CHAdeMO
120kW-140kW	360-560	580-900	Tesla v2 Supercharger
250kW	750-1000	1200-1600	Tesla v3 Supercharger
100kW-350kW	300-1400	480-2250	CCS Ultra Chargers

Table showing the charging speed (miles/hour) for the various charging connectors available in the UK today. All of these connector speeds have a role with BEVs albeit the 43kW connector is now only relevant to one legacy car, no current EVs use it. Only one current BEV uses 22kW, with most 3-phase charging now at 11kW. One EV can charge up to 16.5kW on a 22kW connection. Tesla v2 and v3 Superchargers are currently being converted to CCS configuration.

Combustion Free Mobility for Plymouth

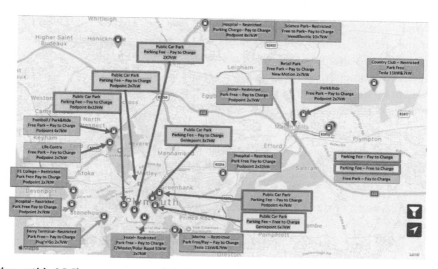

Plymouth's AC Chargers are mostly in high cost car parks with an hourly fee for charging. Park and Ride have free parking but again an hourly fee for charging. Only one car park has free to use chargers. Other chargers are in sites of restricted access. Utilisation of chargers in Plymouth is very low compared to many other parts of the country.

Roadside EV charging – not in expensive car parks! (Photo drive-green.co.uk)

7.61   Plymouth car parks are expensive if you need to use them, but if you only want to charge and not to shop then they double the cost per mile of your driving. If you do park, then you also have to pay £1/hour whilst connected to the charger. For anyone working in Plymouth, charging at 24-40 miles/hour, means that a full day's charge isn't likely to be necessary but moving your car after an hour or two isn't feasible. Other cities allow connection all day with either free power or a charge per kWh only.

7.62   More rapid chargers (>50kW) are also required in and around the city (free to access, pay to use) in a similar fashion to places such as Milton Keynes and Poole. To encourage and incentivise zero emission BEVs, charging rules need to be conducive to their use and make EV ownership a benefit not a problem.

7.63   For BEV drivers who don't have access to home charging, three strategies are required:

   a.   if the battery capacity/range is sufficient, then the car can be treated much like an CEV, recharging when the charge level drops to 20% - this requires sufficient rapid charger hubs to be available near to home and probably a realistic range of 200miles+ and the opportunity for occasional off-street overnight or daytime plugged-in time; or

   b.   opportunity destination/workplace charging or 'grazing' as it is sometimes described, where a charge is taken wherever possible regardless of whether the battery is fully recharged or not – given the low average mileage of many drivers this will work perfectly well for many but not for all.

   c.   On-street charging by pop-up chargers, lamp post outlets, or cross-pavement arrangements, or other such things.

7.64   Based on a Great Britain wide study by the RAC Foundation, 67% of households have garage or off-street parking, 18% have adequate on-street parking and 15% have inadequate off-street parking. The study wasn't carried out to identify the suitability for BEV charging but we can perhaps take it as a guide to the likely ability to achieve home charging and on this basis maybe 15-20% would have difficulties with at home charging depending on the acceptability of the solutions for adequate on street parking.[84]

7.65   For those without off-street parking, there are solutions that can enable BEV ownership. These include lamppost charging (daytime and selected times at night), cross footpath charging, pop-up chargers, and charge bays.

7.66   EV charging from lampposts is growing in popularity[85]. Ubricity have installed more than 1,000 lamppost charge points throughout many towns and cities in the UK.[86] Lampposts typically use a single phase off a three-phase circuit and allow around 20A/4.5kW, when the light is not in use. Many authorities now turn off street lighting between 1am and 5am, or similar low use times, in low risk areas, so this should allow some night-time charging[87]. Ubricity also indicate that with some installations they can go as high as 25A/5.8kW single-phase.

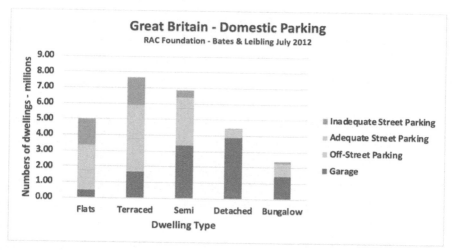

Domestic parking arrangements for Great Britain (RAC Foundation 2012). Based on this, probably around two-thirds to 85% of dwellings could achieve home charging.

Charging from lampposts – (photo drive-green.co.uk)

.67   Other local authorities have addressed the cross-pavement charging issue with different solutions.

.68   Hampshire County Council have adopted rubber cable mats and accepted the difficulties with pushchairs and the like. [88]

Hampshire's accepted solution for on-road EV charging subject to other parking restrictions and no obstruction of footway or access
(Photo Hampshire County Council)

7.69 Oxford have cut channels across the pavement. Users of this scheme report that provided a 'controlled parking zone' is also introduced that the solution works for them most of the time. It's a neat and simple arrangement and, for Oxford, was preferable to lamppost charging.[89]

Oxford's cross-pavement cable channel system for off-street EV charging – a very neat and practical solution in conjunction with a Controlled Parking Zone CPZ.
(Photo: Jesper Ekelund)

7.70 There is a need for a number of high-power rapid charger hubs spaced around the city. These should offer 30-50 charge points with some at 250-350kW, and others at 150kW.

More 30-50 rapid charge point stations capable of delivering 250 miles in 15 minutes are required.

7.71 For Apartments or Flats there are a significant number that have on-street parking and, depending upon the size of the apartment block, providing charge points can be quite challenging.

7.72 For apartments with off-street parking, garage or courtyard, landlords can be quite difficult to convince but many are increasingly seeing the future benefit in retaining the value of their properties as more and more tenants are wanting to adopt EVs.

7.73 The Government's "current EVHS support for owner occupied single unit housing will continue until 31 March 2022 after which date support will focus solely on rental and leasehold properties." The fund will provide landowners/managing companies up to 75% of the cost of retrofit installation of cabling (and any associated connections and communications) needed for installing 7kW (or higher) chargepoints in at least 80% of the spaces in the carpark of a multiunit residential property. The cost of installing chargepoints may be redeemed using the EVHS chargepoint installation fund, this may be concurrent with the ducting work, subsequent or both. The scheme will probably initially be limited to larger multiunit buildings, having 5 or more units and capped at a maximum of £6,500 per carpark and 10 carparks per linked enterprise. [90]

7.74. However, in some cases, there is a physical constraint to the amount of electrical supply available for charging points. Running feeds direct from the tenant's supply is often difficult and the power distribution company would have difficulties with so many EV chargers in one block. Using the landlord's supply can be feasible as there is often some capacity headroom in the supply, but a power management system is necessary if the greatest number of charge points are to be provided.

7.75 There are companies that produce power managed power array that use a three phase 100A/23kW per phase supply to provide 27 charge points at a max of 32A/7.4kW each. On the basis that not all cars will require the full charge all the time, the system charges all up to the maximum of 32A until the maximum is reached when it then sheds load evenly until the minimum of 14A/3.2kW per vehicle is reached [91]. The system works well and as many Tesla owners charging regularly at 3kW can attest, this charge level is perfectly adequate for most users.

7.76 For new apartment blocks, planning consent should be contingent upon all spaces being provided with a power managed EV charging system. This system is much preferable to providing only a few charging points per apartment block.

7.77 The power management system will control the charging with the fee being collected by the charge provider before being passed to the building manager – the landlord need not be involved.

Electric Vehicles can be charged in apartments, but the process to install a charger is inordinately complex and very expensive (Photo David Bricknell)

7.78 Further incentives are also required if rapid uptake of the EVs are to be achieved - these include some or all:

    a. free parking,

    b. access to bus and high occupancy lanes, and

    c. free bridge and ferry tolls.

7.79 There may well be a view expressed that these incentives are not required for people that can afford an EV in the first place. However, in order to ensure sufficient new cars are purchased to provide future affordable second user cars, every incentive is important. Such incentives have helped to achieve significant EV uptake in the cities that have adopted them.

7.80   92

Utility Vans Trucks

7.81 Not to be forgotten are the key utility trucks and delivery vans. Such vehicles will also benefit from zero-emission.

7.82 Delivery vans adapted from EV cars are increasingly becoming available. They are expensive capital items that spend long times at slow speed with considerable power taken by on-board functions – perfect for electric propulsion.

7.83 The significantly lower operating costs and social costs provide a good return on the investment. [93], [94]

7.84 PCC should aim to progressively phase out 'last mile' deliveries by fossil-fuel light vans, transitioning to zero-emission deliveries within the city.[95]

7.85 Our cities will be overwhelmed by unregulated high emission older 'white-vans' if action is not taken at a time when internet shopping is increasing exponentially; [96]

Electric Delivery Vans are available now

(Photo – Clockwise from Top left - Arrival, DHL StreetScooter, Voltia, E-Ducato)

Aviation

7.86 Plymouth no longer has a functioning airport. Electric aircraft are in their infancy, but some forward-looking countries are looking to electrify all internal flights by 2040 - ambitious but achievable.

7.87 In the near term these internal flights are most likely to be with a greater number of smaller 9-seater type battery planes, with up to 150 seat planes coming later[97].

7.88 These airplane types may well suit a revitalised Plymouth airport, being capable of taking passengers on flights of 50-200 miles perhaps some time before 2040. Encouragement should be given to such an ambition.

Zero-emission electric aeroplanes are in their infancy

(Photos MagniX and Matti Blume CC BY-SA 4.0)

PLYMOUTH RESPONSE TO EV OWNERSHIP

8. Plymouth response to EV Ownership

8.1 Plymouth can contribute to the increased adoption of EVs over and above the incentives introduced by central government.

8.2 Plymouth City Council's Transport and Planning Officer states[98]:[99]

8.2.1 With regards to off-street parking - "There are of course some properties in Plymouth where there is limited off-street which makes this more challenging and **this would of course need to be factored into any decision by an individual to purchase and electric car"**

8.2.2 With regards to car park charges and fee for charging - "Most cars would be fully charged within 4 hours. Even doing this three-times a week it makes it competitive with filling up a conventional fuelled car at a petrol station. **The parking charge (in a centre car park) is irrelevant as anyone parking in the public car parks would have to pay this.**"

8.2.3 With regards to apartments – "The Council cannot compel existing property owners to install charging facilities for electric cars". "OLEV funding reduces the cost of their 7kW charge point from £859 to £359" (Note: installing an EV Charger in an apartment cost nearer £2,000).

8.2.4 Publicly available charge points "have been installed at many of the city's key destinations including city centre, the city's park and ride sites, Derriford and Mount Gould Hospitals, Plymouth Life Centre and City College" **"what people do with their time whilst their car is charging is obviously a personal choice".**

8.2.5 "The major oil companies … are planning to install charge points … **making refuelling electric cars akin to the way combustion cars do at the moment."**

8.2.6 PCC seem rather unsympathetic to EV driving and lack an understanding of what is necessary to 'drive electric'.

MARINE EMISSIONS

9. Marine emissions

Marine Emissions are significant and affect the city as well as Plymouth Sound

Plymouth Port, Management and Oversight

9.1 As with all ports, significant amounts of emissions from marine traffic can affect the city. A Considerable volume of marine traffic travel through Plymouth Sound into the Cattewater and Millbay Docks as well as to the Naval Dockyard and the Estuaries. This traffic continues throughout the year, day and night.

9.2 Plymouth port "handles over 2 million tonnes of cargo per year, in addition to regular Brittany Ferries services to Roscoff and Santander, and cruise ship visits landing at Millbay Docks and the Barbican".

9.3 The Port of Plymouth is controlled by the Queens Harbour Master (QHM), an independent authority accountable to the Secretary of State for Defence for the protection of the Port of Plymouth, including protecting the environment. [100]

9.4 The Tamar Estuaries Consultative Forum (TECF) is a collaboration between the different authorities that use the Port. It is chaired by the Queen's Harbour Master and hosted by Plymouth City Council.

9.5 Other authorities, part of the TECF, include Associated British Ports, Cattewater Harbour Commissioners, Devon County Council, Devon and Severn Inshore Fisheries and Conservation Authorities, Cornwall County Council, Cornwall Inshore Fisheries and Conservation Authorities, Defence Infrastructure Organisation, Duchy of Cornwall, Sutton Harbour, Tamar Valley Area of Outstanding Natural Beauty, and West Devon Borough Council. [101]

9.6 Cattewater Harbour Commissioners (CHC) exists by an Act of Parliament as the navigation and conservancy authority for the Cattewater Harbour, as well as civil pilotage authority for the Port of Plymouth." [102]

9.7 Plymouth Pilotage Service saw 997 shipping moves in 2018, consisting of ferries, tankers, coasters and specialist vessels in and out of Cattedown, Corporation and Victoria Wharves, and Millbay Docks."

9.8 Approximately 59% of marine cargo into Plymouth is Petroleum, something that will be time limited as fossil fuel use inevitably declines. [103]

Marine designations and regulations

9.9   The Plymouth Sound and Tamar Estuaries Marine Protected Area (MPA) includes a Special Area of Conservation (SAC), a Special Protection Area SPA and a Marine Conservation Zone (MCZ). These are legally designated under various European Union Directives.

9.10 Within the Port of Plymouth are MCA categorised Inland Waterways – Cat C (from Mountbatten Pier through Drake's Island to Raveness Point) and Cat D (Cawsand to Breakwater to Staddon).

9.11 Inland Waterways vessels are required to meet EU non-road emissions standards. The latest Stage V requirements more closely align to the on-road Euro 6d requirements in requiring NOx emission control and a Particulate Filter. Standards are less onerous on older vessels.

9.12 It is recommended that older vessels are either updated to meet Stage V or restricted in port access in a similar manner to the way older motor vehicles should be restricted from the city centre.

9.13 According to the National Atmospheric Emissions Inventory (NAEI), emissions from domestic shipping (ships that start and end their journey in the UK) accounted for 10% of the UK's total domestic NO_x emissions, 2% of $PM_{2.5}$ and 7% of SO2 in 2016. Given that Plymouth is a significant port, the proportional impact of shipping on the town will be therefore relatively higher than the UK national average. [104]

9.14 Domestic vessels and International vessels (>500GRT) are required to comply with International Maritime Organisation rules and to meet the requirements of The International Convention for the Prevention of Pollution from Ships (MARPOL) regulations. For emissions this is Annex VI – Prevention of Air Pollution from Ships.

9.15 International marine traffic, which is the bulk of ferry and cargo traffic for Plymouth, will be a much larger contributor of emissions.

9.16 IMO emission levels apply to **NOx, Particulates and to Sulphur Oxides SOx**.

9.17 For NOx, emission levels have reduced since IMO I was introduced in 1990 with Tier II applying from year 2000. Tier III are the most stringent but are only being applied in **(NOx) Emission Control Areas ECA** which does not include the English Channel, so Plymouth is left with rather polluting Tier II NOx standards.

9.18 A **Sulphur Control Area SECA** is in operation through the Channel to just east of the port of Falmouth and is in force from 2020.

9.19 From 2020, ships are required to use low sulphur fuels. An 'acceptable alternative' sometimes described as a 'legal loophole' allows them to continue to use high sulphur fuels provided they use Exhaust Gas Cleaning (EGC), also known as 'scrubbers'. Scrubbers wash the toxic emissions from the exhaust fumes, thereby meeting air emission regulations, and send the highly acidic wash water straight into the surrounding water thereby shortcutting the air emission but still polluting the oceans.

Cattewater and Millbay Docks

9.20 The Cattewater Harbour Commissioners CHC, together with Plymouth Marine Laboratory, indicate that 95% (by number of vessels over 500grt,) use low sulphur fuel.

9.21 CHC require any ships entering the Cattewater to switch to closed-loop scrubber operation retaining the wash-water on board. CHC regularly monitor air quality in the Cattewater with a sensor on Breakwater Hill.

9.22 CHC do not enforce the IMO 2020 regulation. That Statutory duty resides with the Maritime and Coastguard Agency MCA.

9.23 Associated British Ports ABP monitor air quality around Millbay Docks. They have set no regulation on the ships entering and leaving Millbay for scrubbers to be used in 'Closed-Loop' mode. Closed Loop mode should be the minimum standard for operation within Plymouth Port.

9.24 Most domestic marine traffic will be a few hundred kW of power whereas the cross-channel ferries could be around 40,000kW or about 2,000times more power. [105]

Cross Channel Ferry turning towards Millbay Docks – (Photo David Bricknell)

Cold Ironing

9.25   In addition to sulphur, the issues remain around GHGs (CO_2 and Methane) and toxic emissions. Brittany Ferries are now planning to fit some of the ferries to use LNG fuel which while reducing CO_2 can increase the GHG (Methane) emissions. Particulates will be reduced. [106]

9.26   As well as emissions from sailing into and out of the port including manoeuvring, large cargo ships tend to use their on-board generators whilst at their berth as well as when on a buoy or at anchor. At berth the option to plug into shore power, and hence turn off polluting diesel generators, should be made a requirement - this is known as cold ironing - and can make a considerable impact on reducing marine emissions. [107]

Cold Ironing, shore power to ships at berth, is essential to reducing marine emissions (Photo brighthubengineering)

9.27   Without cold-ironing, consideration should also be given to requiring all vessels to only operate Stage V approved generator sets when within the port and at berth

Electric Ships

9.28 Plymouth's Action Plan makes mention of a new electric ferry charger infrastructure at the Barbican which, one assumes, is either for the council-run Mountbatten Ferry or for the new EV for Plymouth Boat Trips. This would be a small step forward and, as the rest of the marine traffic is in the control of CHC, is the best that PCC can do. We look forward to that ferry but would hope that many other harbour ferries and tour boats could also become electric in the near future. [108]

Movitz, Stockholm's Electric Harbour Ferry, and Green City Ferries BB Green Fast Ferry

9.29 CHC say "We will commit to reviewing our Marine Assets at the end of their working life, and where possible, replace with newer, low emission models where practical. We will also monitor the development of hybrid engine technology on small marine craft and assess its feasibility for our own assets."

9.30 The working life of marine craft can be anything from 15-40 years, so this is rather a weak ambition and certainly not sufficient to meet climate aims.

9.31 Authorities around the UK are already replacing pilot vessels with hybrid propulsion. [109]

9.32 Large ferry operators are already adopting propulsion arrangements that allow emission free operations.

Denmark's Ellen [110] Inter-Island Car-Passenger Ro-Pax Ferry carrying 200 passengers and 30 cars - 4.3MWh battery pack, and M/F Tycho Brahe[111] carrying 1250 passengers, 260 trucks, 240 cars and 9 passenger train coaches - 4MWh battery pack (Photo News Oresund CC-by-2.0).

Marine Summary

9.33 Plymouth should aim to be combustion-free within Plymouth Sound and its Estuaries by 2030 – the technology is available.

9.34 It is recommended that older Inland Waterway vessels are either updated to meet Stage V emission regulations or restricted in port access in a similar manner to the way older motor vehicles should be restricted from the city centre.

9.35 It is recommended that all vessels operating within Plymouth Sound and its Estuaries are required to use Low Sulphur Fuel or where Exhaust Gas Cleaning (Scrubbers) are used then they are required to be operated in Closed Loop mode.

9.36 Marine Air Pollution monitoring should be available real-time to all Plymouth residents.

9.37 Cold-Ironing / Shore Power should be mandatory in the Cattewater and Millbay Docks as it is within the Naval dockyard.

9.38 Where shore power is not provided, ships berthed should be required to use on-board generators that meet EU Stage V emission standards.

9.39 Plymouth should encourage, and incentivise where possible, the introduction of battery-electric harbour vessels and battery (or zero-emission) operation for all vessels within Plymouth Sound.

COMMITMENT

10. Commitment

10.1 Climate Action Plymouth will actively campaign for and support initiatives that lead to the implementation of measures that will result in Plymouth reaching its target of net zero emissions by or before 2030.

10.2 We urge Plymouth City Council to take all possible measures to put into place the recommendations above with regard to mobility on both land and water.

10.3 Members of the Transport Working Group of Climate Action Plymouth.

David Bricknell **CEng, FRINA, BSc (Hons)** Naval Architect and Marine Engineer, specialist in Power and Propulsion, author of five books on the Electric Vehicle revolution.

Pat Bushell Cyclist

Dr Michael Littledyke **BSc, MEd, PhD, PGCE, Adv Dip [drama] in Ed**, Senior Fellow of the Higher Education Academy [specialism in education for science and sustainability]. University of New England (Associate Professor), NSW, Australia and University of Gloucestershire, UK (Principal Lecturer).

Ricky Lowes, **M.A.,** Senior Fellow of the Higher Education Academy

Tony Staunton **BA (Hons 1st),** President, Plymouth TUC; accredited Green Rep; National Steering Group - Campaign against Climate Change.

FUD - FAQS

11. FUD – FAQs

11.1 Accompanying discussions on climate change are the inevitable statements of Fear, Uncertainty, and Doubt, sown to deflect the argument from the solutions. These capture some of the usual suspects.

11.2 Electric Vehicles EVs are as dirty as combustion engine vehicles – FALSE. The electricity grid in the UK delivers energy from three major sources - renewables and gas with some nuclear. Using emission limits on power stations points to an BEV's energy producing about a third of the emissions on an CEV but crucially at the point of use it is zero emission. As the grid gets cleaner, so will the BEV. Of course, if you charge directly from solar, wind or hydro then you will be zero emission.

11.3 EVs are too expensive compared to CEV – FALSE. All new cars are expensive; EVs fall within the range of prices on combustion engine cars albeit nearer the top end of the model variants – once the OLEV grant has been taken into account. Cheaper, second hand EVs will only be available once the new car is purchased.

11.4 EVs produce more particulates from brakes and tyres than CEV vehicles because they are heavier – FALSE. This view came from an older report when BEVs were heavier than CEV and were limited in their energy regeneration. Today, a purpose designed BEV is similar in weight to the equivalent CEV, regeneration capability means brakes are rarely used, and smoother acceleration and braking means tyres last longer.

11.5 Batteries need replacing every two years - FALSE. EV batteries will deteriorate from usage and age and the rate they deteriorate will be influenced by temperature and depth of discharge. Today's batteries are carefully temperature controlled and of large capacity, so discharge is lower than with a smaller battery pack. EV batteries carry an eight or sometimes a ten-year warranty and between 100,000 to 160,000mile use warranty. The expectation of a 2019 battery would be 250,000 to 500,000miles and one manufacturer is promising a million-mile battery in the near future. Battery packs were originally designed for rapid change but are now designed closely integral to the vehicle structure so the confidence in battery life is clearly high.

11.6 BEVs take too long to charge – FALSE. Compared to refilling a petrol or diesel tank, the BEV can either take less time or more time. Most EV recharging means plugging in for an overnight charge – this takes less of the owner's time than driving to a refuelling station. Overnight charging at home is around 25 miles per hour of charge so an eight hour overnight or daytime charge would prove 200 miles or a full battery whichever is first. On-route charging is now available up to 250 miles in 15-minutes, plenty quick enough for a long-distance trip.

11.7 BEVs run out of fuel regularly – FALSE. Proportionally CEV vehicles run out of fuel more times than BEVs run out of charge.

1.8   BEVs catch fire easily – FALSE. BEVs have proportionally fewer vehicle fires than CEV.

1.9   BEVs use batteries that are environmentally damaging. - FALSE for many BEV manufactures but TRUE for some. The 'environmentally damaging' comment refers to lithium. Although lithium is the descriptor for a Li-Ion battery they contain very little lithium ~ about 2% by volume of lithium in an BEV battery. BEV Lithium-Ion batteries are composed predominantly of nickel and graphite. Lithium can be extracted from salts in a process that uses lots of water and is seen as environmentally damaging, but lithium can also be extracted from hard rock; the largest BEV manufacturers use lithium from hard rock extraction.

1.10 BEV batteries use cobalt that is extracted using child labour. FALSE for many BEV manufactures but TRUE for some. The 'child-labour' comment refers to cobalt and is related to the use of artisanal mining in the Democratic Republic of Congo DRC, sometimes involving children. Consumer electronics use a Li-Ion battery with a cathode composed of about 50% cobalt whereas BEV batteries are either less than 10% or zero. Major BEV manufacturers are mostly sourcing their cobalt from countries other than the DRC. In summary, neither lithium nor cobalt are major constituents of an EV battery and most major manufacturers avoid sourcing these materials from countries that pose these problems. For information, cobalt is also used for desulphurisation of petrol/diesel fuel and in producing recyclable plastics as well as in glass, porcelain, ceramics, paints, inks and enamelware amongst many other daily use products.

1.11 BEVs can't drive in the wet – FALSE. There are no restrictions on EV driving weather conditions. Both CEV and BEVs will suffer from extremely low temperatures (approx. minus 40°C)

1.12 People with pacemakers can't drive in a BEV – FALSE. There are no restrictions on pacemakers with BEVs.

1.13 EVs can't drive far in the winter – FALSE. All vehicles get reduced range from higher air density, colder tyres, rain and standing water – these are the same for EVs as CEV. CEVs use waste heat for the cabin whereas BEVs use battery energy. This does have an impact but waste heat recovery from motor and electronics and heat pumps have now minimised the impact.

1.14 BEVs are so slow – FALSE. BEVs now have the world's quickest saloon cars.

1.15 There aren't enough chargers – TRUE but the situation is improving rapidly. There are now more BEV chargers than there are fuel pumps. Many towns and cities have addressed the situation to provide a wide variety of chargers throughout the city. Major route rapid charging network is rapidly growing.

1.16 There is not enough power generation available to power BEVs – FALSE. The National Grid consider that the situation is manageable. BEVs can charge off-peak and with the future renewables this will be at night and middle of the day. Avoiding charging at commuting times morning and evening ensures plenty of power will be available.

11.17 Charge points aren't always available where buses and BEVs want to charge - TRUE. This can be a problem but requires effort to solve the problems with both the National Grid and the local power distribution companies. Wayleaves, or rights of way, need specific attention but there are few technical issues.

REFERENCES

12. References

[1] The Buchanan Report: Traffic in Towns https://api.parliament.uk/historic-hansard/lords/1963/nov/27/the-buchanan-report-traffic-in-towns

[2] How Surface transport could be decarbonised by regulation – Steve Melia, UWE
https://www.youtube.com/watch?v=IPMemflhuwo

[3] Norway and the A-ha moment that became electric cars the answer - drivethecars
http://www.drivethecars.net/norway-and-the-a-ha-moment-that-made-electric-cars-the-answer-8/

[4] Transport Secretary's statement on coronavirus (COVID-19): 9 May 2020
https://www.gov.uk/government/speeches/transport-secretarys-statement-on-coronavirus-covid-19-9-may-2020

[5] Plymouth City Council wins emergency DfT funding for active travel plans – smart transport
https://www.smarttransport.org.uk/news/latest-news/plymouth-city-council-wins-emergency-funding-for-active-travel-plans

[6] 2018 Greenhouse Gas Emissions, provisional figures - Statistical Release: National Statistics
https://assets.publishing.service.gov.uk/government/uploads/system/uploads/attachment_data/file/790626/2018-provisional-emissions-statistics-report.pdf

[7] Climate Emergency Public Consultation
https://www.plymouth.gov.uk/environmentandpollution/climatechangeandenergy/climateemergencypublicconsultation

[8] How – Certified Carbon Neutral Global Standard https://www.carbonneutral.com/how
[9] Global Heating: best and worst case scenarios less likely than thought – The Guardian
https://www.theguardian.com/environment/2020/jul/22/global-heating-study-narrows-range-of-probable-temperature-rises

[10] Analysis: Why the UK's CO2 emissions have fallen 38% since 1990 – Carbon Brief, Clear on Climate
https://www.carbonbrief.org/analysis-why-the-uks-co2-emissions-have-fallen-38-since-1990

[11] UK approval for biggest gas power station in Europe ruled legal – The Guardian
https://www.theguardian.com/environment/2020/may/22/uk-approval-for-biggest-gas-power-station-europe-ruled-legal-high-court-climate-planning

[12] Britain now G7's biggest net importer of CO2 emissions per capita , says ONS – The Guardian
https://www.theguardian.com/uk-news/2019/oct/21/britain-is-g7s-biggest-net-importer-of-co2-emissions-per-capita-says-ons

[13] Scotland must 'walk the talk' on climate change – BBC News https://www.bbc.co.uk/news/uk-scotland-50808243

[14] 15m people in the UK live in areas of dangerously high pollution – are you among them? INews
https://inews.co.uk/news/environment/high-air-pollution-uk-areas-revealed-1384137

[15] Plan to ban petrol and diesel cars by 2035 is 'extremely concerning' warns UK motor industry – The Times https://www.driving.co.uk/news/plan-ban-petrol-diesel-cars-2035-extremely-concerning-warns-uk-motor-industry/

[16] Coronavirus vaccine: When will we have one? – BBC News https://www.bbc.co.uk/news/health-51665497

[17] Global Warming Potentials (IPCC Second Assessment Report) (https://unfccc.int/process/transparency-and-reporting/greenhouse-gas-data/greenhouse-gas-data-unfccc/global-warming-potentials).

[18] Transport Energy Model – Report: Moving Britain Ahead – UK Department of Transport

[19] Emissions from bus travel – carbon Independent https://www.carbonindependent.org/20.html

[20] Airborne particulate matter and their health effects – Encyclopedia of the Environment https://www.encyclopedie-environnement.org/en/health/airborne-particulate-health-effects/

[21] National Air Quality Testing Services https://www.naqts.com/whats-in-your-air/particles/

[22] Reports and statements from the Committee on the Medical Effects of Air Pollutants (COMEAP). https://www.gov.uk/government/collections/comeap-reports

[23] Brake, tyre and road surface wear call for evidence: summary of responses.July 2019 https://www.gov.uk/government/consultations/air-quality-brake-tyre-and-road-surface-wear-call-for-evidence/outcome/brake-tyre-and-road-surface-wear-call-for-evidence-summary-of-responses

[24] Particulate Matter Measurements, Burtscher and Majewski https://dieselnet.com/tech/measure_dpm.php

[25] Diesel car particulate emissions spike up to 115% during DPF cleaning – Richard Aucock Motoring Research https://www.motoringresearch.com/car-news/diesel-car-particulate-emissions-spike/

[26] Briefing paper on non-exhaust particulate emissions from road transport – Transport Research Laboratory http://www.lowemissionstrategies.org/downloads/Jan15/Non_Exhaust_Particles11.pdf)

[27] WHO limits for particulate matter will be enshrined in UK law, pledges Gove – air quality news (https://airqualitynews.com/2019/07/16/who-limits-for-particulate-matter-will-be-enshrined-in-uk-law-pledges-gove/)

[28] Plymouth's polluted air is dangerous to breathe, World Health Organisation report claims – Plymouth Live (https://www.plymouthherald.co.uk/news/health/plymouths-polluted-air-dangerous-breathe-704029)

[29] Dangerous ultra-fine particles from diesel cars 'ignored' by law – air quality news https://airqualitynews.com/2020/02/26/dangerous-ultra-fine-particles-from-diesel-cars-ignored-by-the-law/

[30] Brewery CO2 Monitor https://www.co2meter.com/blogs/news/brewery-co2-monitor

[31] The real story of the canary in the coal mine https://www.smithsonianmag.com/smart-news/story-real-canary-coal-mine-180961570/

[32] Plymouth worse than London for air pollution – World Health Organisation - Plymouth Live https://www.plymouthherald.co.uk/news/plymouth-worse-london-air-pollution-1523721

- [33] WHO Global Urban Ambient Air Pollution Database (update 2016) Ambient (outdoor) air pollution database, by country and city
xlsx, 1.31Mb

[34] Plymouth City Council Air Quality Plan https://www.plymouth.gov.uk/airqualityactionplan

[35] Hambleton, Robin - Leading the healthy city: taking advantage of the power of place.

[36] Children in the urban environment: an issue for the new public health agenda   - Davis and Jones https://www.sciencedirect.com/science/article/abs/pii/1353829296000032

[37] 20-minute Neighbourhoods – Plan Melbourne https://www.planmelbourne.vic.gov.au/current-projects/20-minute-neighbourhoods

[38] Cycling Revolution London – Transport for London https://www.london.gov.uk/sites/default/files/cycling-revolution-london.pdf

[39] Britain's potential cyclists put off cycling due to traffic conditions and potholes – Cycling UK https://www.cyclinguk.org/press-release/britains-potential-cyclists-put-cycling-due-traffic-conditions-and-potholes

[40] Pollutionwatch: how bike roads can reduce exposure to toxic air – Gary Fuller https://www.theguardian.com/environment/2020/may/21/pollutionwatch-how-bike-roads-can-reduce-exposure-to-toxic-air

[41] Norman Foster unveils plans for elevated 'Skycycle' bike routes in London https://www.theguardian.com/artanddesign/architecture-design-blog/2014/jan/02/norman-foster-skycycle-elevated-bike-routes-london

[42] The effect of hills on cycling http://www.aviewfromthecyclepath.com/2009/10/effect-of-hills-on-cycling.html

[43] E-Scooters set to be trialled on the UK roads as government consults on rules to make them legal https://www.standard.co.uk/news/transport/escooters-trial-uk-roads-a4387871.html

[44] On demand electric bike hire in Exeter https://www.co-bikes.co.uk

[45] Sainsbury's to trial 'UK first' South London electric cargo bike delivery fleet. https://www.commercialfleet.org/news/latest-news/2018/04/23/sainsbury-s-to-trial-uk-first-south-london-electric-cargo-bike-delivery-fleet

[46] Plans for new roads threaten Bristol's countryside and limit action on the climate crisis – Steve Melia https://thebristolcable.org/2020/01/plans-for-new-road-threaten-bristols-countryside-and-undo-action-on-the-climate-crisis/

[47] Public energy consumption investigation for transition to electric power and semi-dynamic charging – Graurs, Laizans, Rajeckis, Rubenis – Transport and Telecommunications Institute, Latvia University http://www.tf.llu.lv/conference/proceedings2015/Papers/060_Graurs.pdf

[48] Coronavirus (COVID-19): safer travel guidance for passengers – walking, cycling and travelling in vehicles or

on public transport during the coronavirus outbreak – Department of Transport
https://www.gov.uk/guidance/coronavirus-covid-19-safer-travel-guidance-for-passengers#public-transport

[49] Emissions from bus travel – Carbon Independent https://www.carbonindependent.org/20.html

[50] Back to work : Capacity of transport network will be down by 90% - Grant Shapps
https://www.theguardian.com/world/2020/may/09/back-to-work-capacity-of-transport-network-will-be-down-by-90

[51] Coronavirus (COVID-19): safer travel guidance for passengers – walking, cycling and travelling in vehicles or on public transport during the coronavirus outbreak – Department of Transport
https://www.gov.uk/guidance/coronavirus-covid-19-safer-travel-guidance-for-passengers#public-transport

[52] Massively unfair gulf in bus fares between London and rest of England – The Guardian
https://www.theguardian.com/uk-news/2019/may/05/bus-fares-reveal-massively-unfair-gulf-between-london-and-rest-of-england

[53] Manchester's mayor considers taking back control of buses – The Economist
https://www.economist.com/britain/2019/02/02/manchesters-mayor-considers-taking-back-control-of-buses

[54] London congestion charge https://enacademic.com/dic.nsf/enwiki/120702

[55] Urban transport without the hot air – Steve Melia http://www.stevemelia.co.uk/urbantransport.html

[56] http://www.stevemelia.co.uk/urbantransport.html

[57] Electric vs Diesel vs Natural Gas: which bus is best for the climate – Union of Concerned Scientists
https://blog.ucsusa.org/jimmy-odea/electric-vs-diesel-vs-natural-gas-which-bus-is-best-for-the-climate.

[58] Particle and gaseous emissions from compressed natural gas and ultralow sulphur diesel-fuelled buses at four steady engine loads – Jayaratne, Ristovski, Meyer, Morawska.
https://www.sciencedirect.com/science/article/pii/S0048969709000102.

[59] London's electric bus fleet expands – air quality news - https://airqualitynews.com/2018/02/15/londons-electric-bus-fleet-expands/

[60] Electric buses to take over Sydney https://transportnsw.wordpress.com/2019/10/28/electric-buses-to-take-over-sydney/

[61] Plymouth gets its first electric bus – but you won't be able to ride it Plymouth Live.
(https://www.plymouthherald.co.uk/news/business/plymouth-gets-first-electric-bus-2972046).

[62]
http://www.byd.com/sites/Satellite?c=BydArticle&cid=1502366110168&d=Touch&pagename=BYD_EN%2FBydArticle%2FBYD_ENCommon%2FArticleDetails

[63] Buses: Government unveils £50m plan to create first all-electric bus town – BBC News
https://www.bbc.co.uk/news/business-51391764

[64] https://cleantechnica.com/2018/04/29/no-need-to-wait-electric-buses-are-cost-competitive-transit-buses-

today/

[65] No need to wait: Electric buses are cost competitive transit buses today - Cleantechnica http://www.chinabuses.org/news/2011/0121/article_4019.html.

[66] MetroCentro - Andalusia, Spain https://en.wikipedia.org/wiki/MetroCentro_(Seville)

[67] London Atmospheric Emissions Inventory (LAEI) 2010 (https://data.london.gov.uk/dataset/london-atmospheric-emissions-inventory-2010)

[68] Alstom to deliver its first battery electric trains – InsideEVs https://insideevs.com/news/397585/alstom-first-battery-electric-trains/

[69] TRA0101 Department of Transport Statistics Road traffic (vehicle miles) by vehicle type in Great Britain

[70] London low emissions streets: All you need to know about the first petrol and diesel car ban on east London roads – Evening Standard https://www.standard.co.uk/news/transport/londons-first-ultralow-emissions-streets-everything-you-need-to-know-as-petrol-and-diesel-cars-are-a3923856.html

[71] Plymouth City Council Air Quality Management Area Declaration http://democracy.plymouth.gov.uk/documents/s56951/Air%20Quality%20Management%20Area%20Declaration.pdf

[72] Rise in UK car CO2 emissions largely a result of increasing SUV sales, not declining diesel Transport and Environment https://www.transportenvironment.org/newsroom/blog/rise-uk-car-co2-emissions-largely-result-increasing-suv-sales-not-declining-diesel

[73] Open Consultation ending the sale of new Petrol, diesel and hybrid cars and vans. https://www.gov.uk/government/consultations/consulting-on-ending-the-sale-of-new-petrol-diesel-and-hybrid-cars-and-vans/consulting-on-ending-the-sale-of-new-petrol-diesel-and-hybrid-cars-and-vans?fbclid=IwAR0E7oEG8YooRXCx7R9fcI2ZBr41AgfDnAe3Hu8rXEf4Oubd2wWl_3fnhCA

[74] 2020 Global Automotive Consumer Study https://www2.deloitte.com/us/en/pages/manufacturing/articles/automotive-trends-millennials-consumer-study.html

[75] AM Online New Car Sales Figures https://www.am-online.com/data/manufacturer-insight

[76] Licensed cars by keepership (private and company): Great Britain and United Kingdom

[77] Norwegian EV Policy Norsk elbilforening https://elbil.no/english/norwegian-ev-policy/.

[78] Comparing the top 5 European countries for Electric Vehicle adoption - Fleetcarma https://www.fleetcarma.com/european-countries-electric-vehicle-adoption/

[79] Plug in car Grants UK.Gov https://www.gov.uk/government/news/plug-in-vehicle-grants-update-following-todays-budget

[80] UK has more EV charging stations than petrol – Autocar https://www.autocar.co.uk/car-news/industry/uk-

has-more-ev-charging-stations-petrol-stations

[81] UK has more EV charging stations than petrol stations - Autocar
https://www.statista.com/statistics/312331/number-of-petrol-stations-in-the-united-kingdom-uk/

[82] Stirling MSP calls for help to stem decline in rural petrol stations – Daily Record
https://www.dailyrecord.co.uk/news/local-news/stirling-msp-calls-help-stem-2746780

[83] Understanding Tesla's lithium ion batteries
https://evannex.com/blogs/news/understanding-teslas-lithium-ion-batteries

[84] RAC Foundation – Spaced out: perspectives on parking
policyhttps://www.racfoundation.org/research/mobility/spaced-out-perspectives-on-parking

[85] Motoring Research – Electric Avenue: the first entire street with lamp post car charging
https://www.motoringresearch.com/car-news/electric-avenue-lamp-post-charging/

[86] Ubricity – Intelligent residential on-street charging https://www.ubitricity.co.uk

[87] Essex – Part Night Lighting https://www.essexhighways.org/transport-and-roads/roads-and-pavements/street-lighting/part-night-lighting.aspx

[88] Hampshire County Council Electric vehicle charging – guidance for residents
https://www.hants.gov.uk/transport/ev-charging-points/ev-charging-guidance

[89] Go ultra-low Oxford – eHome Charger and Cable Gully
https://www.goultralowoxford.org/info/5/chargers/13/chargers/3

[90] https://www.smartsurvey.co.uk/s/D4035V/

[91] Podpoint Array Charging https://pod-point.com/products/business/array

[92] Norwegian EV policy: Norway is leading the way for a transition to zero emission in transport – Norsk elbilforening https://elbil.no/english/norwegian-ev-policy/.

[3] https://arrival.com

[4] https://www.dpdhl.com/en/media-relations/specials/electro-mobility.html

[95] https://www.theguardian.com/business/2020/may/20/coronavirus-changing-shopping-habits-forever-says-ms-chief

[96] Electromobility – Deutsche Post DHL Group http://www.urbantransportgroup.org/system/files/general-docs/White%20Van%20Cities.pdf

[97] Easyjet – electric planes by 2030 – Gregory Micallef Associates (https://www.gmal.co.uk/easyjet-electric-planes-by-2030/

[98] Email 26th October 2017 Neil Honey to David Bricknell

[99] Letter 30th August 2018 Neil Honey to Luke Pollard

[100] Queens harbour Master – Gov.uk
https://www.gov.uk/government/organisations/queens-harbour-master/about

[101] Plymouth Sound and Tamar Estuaries http://www.plymouth-mpa.uk

[102] Cattewater Harbour Commissioners https://plymouthport.org.uk

[103] https://plymouthport.org.uk/sites/default/files/Air%20Quality.pdf.

[104] Air pollutant emissions from domestic vessels and inland waterways – A call for evidence – Dept for Transport
https://assets.publishing.service.gov.uk/government/uploads/system/uploads/attachment_data/file/815970/air-pollutant-emissions-from-domestic-vessels-and-inland-waterways-a-call-for-evidence.pdf

[105] Thousands of ships could dump pollutants at sea to avoid dirty fuel ban
https://www.theguardian.com/environment/2018/oct/29/thousands-of-ships-could-dump-pollutants-at-sea-to-avoid-dirty-fuel-ban

[106] Brittany Ferries and the Environment https://www.brittany-ferries.co.uk/information/about/brittany-ferries-and-environment/honfleur

[107] Dunkirk Port switches on Cold Ironing https://www.marinelink.com/news/dunkirk-port-switches-cold-ironing-474434

[108] Green City Ferries – we do high-speed electric ferries http://greencityferries.com

[109] Goodchild Marine's new hybrid pilot vessel is launched – SeaGlaze
http://www.seaglaze.co.uk/uncategorized/case-goodchild-hybrid-pilot/

[110] Denmark's super ferry Ellen takes to the sea – electricdrive
https://www.electrive.com/2019/08/16/powerful-electric-ferry-ellen-takes-to-the-sea/

[111] ForSea battery-electric ferries https://www.forseaferries.com/about-forsea/ferries-and-port/

Printed in Great Britain
by Amazon

33600432R00050